For Hannah 'H.P. Sauce' Pond

The Gospel According To
LITTLE ARTIST BOY

Magda Archer

PIATKUS

PIATKUS

First published in Great Britain in 2021 by Piatkus

1 3 5 7 9 10 8 6 4 2

A CIP catalogue record for this book is available from the British Library.

ISBN: 978-0-349-43111-6

Printed and bound in Italy by L.E.G.O. S.p.A.

Papers used by Piatkus are from well-managed forests and other responsible sources.

Piatkus
An imprint of
Little, Brown Book Group
Carmelite House
50 Victoria Embankment
London EC4Y 0DZ
An Hachette UK Company
www.hachette.co.uk
www.littlebrown.co.uk

CONTENTS

The Gospel According To
LITTLE ARTIST BOY
Introduction

Some years ago, whilst I was holidaying in Montmartre, Paris, I was sitting drinking a café au lait when I heard a small voice …

"Is this seat taken?" it said.

"Why … no," I replied. Looking up, I was confronted by a small figure in a smock and a beret. Childlike, certainly … but was he a man or a child? It was quite impossible to say.

I bought him an Orangina and he told me of his life. One moment I was laughing and the next, I was wiping a tear from my eye.

We must have been there for several hours; time flies in his company.

Eventually he had drunk the last drop from the bottle and, noticing how the shadow of it fell when he returned it to the table, he exclaimed:

"I must move on … au revoir!"

As I watched him wind his way through the pretty streets I reached for my notepad to jot down all that he'd told me.

"Who WAS that?" I asked the waiter.

"That, Mademoiselle," he said with a knowing smile, "was the Little Artist Boy!"

Magda Archer

GRATITUDE
& MINDFUL
LIVING

"Don't be hard
on yourself!
BUT! Don't be soft
on yourself either!
be 'just right'
on yourself,
turns out
Goldilocks was on
to something"

"When it stops and it WILL, you'll miss it" (applies to most things)

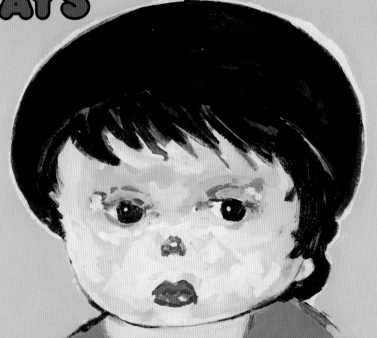

LITTLE ARTIST BOY
SAYS

"AVOID KNOWN IRRITANTS"

LITTLE ARTIST BOY SAYS

"TUNE OUT OF CONVERSATIONS & DAYDREAM TO YOUR HEART'S CONTENT"

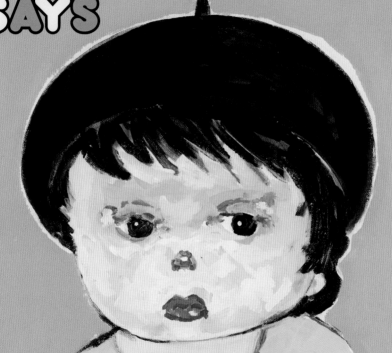

Stop chasing things
that don't exist, like...
UNICORNS
for instance...
I know, I've spoilt it
but someone
HAD to tell you

LITTLE ARTIST BOY SAYS

"Acknowledgement is your best friend, acceptance is your second best friend"

LITTLE ARTIST BOY SAYS

"MORE DOUGHNUTS PLEASE!"

KEEPING THE MIND SHARP & THE BRAIN TRAINED

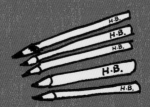

"IF IT LOOKS LIKE ART, IT PROBABLY IS ART... IF IT DOESN'T LOOK LIKE ART, IT MOST PROBABLY IS ART"

LITTLE ARTIST BOY

"NOTHING IS QUITE
WHAT IT SEEMS"

"That person,
'Ms X' seemed shifty
& grasping to me"
"That person,
'Mr X' sends very
negative texts"
Observation & Detective
work are good but you
will need a notebook
& a biro or H.B. pencil

LITTLE ARTIST BOY SAYS

"Shut up about being invisible!, hang on, just a moment where've you got to?"

LITTLE ARTIST BOY SAYS

"Talking of fashion ... fashion connects current thinking to every day life, so ... DON'T KNOCK IT!"

FINANCES, WORK, DRUDGERY

"WHEN YOU MESS UP...
BE THE FIRST TO SAY IT...
OR, MAYBE THE SECOND...
OR, JUST SAY IT AT SOME
POINT WHEN THINGS
ARE GOING RAPIDLY
DOWNHILL"

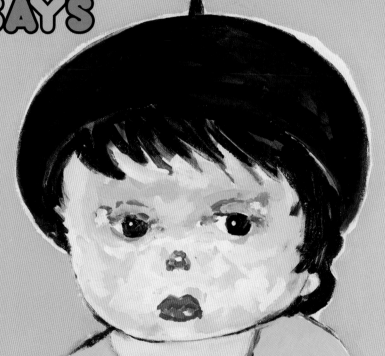

LITTLE ARTIST BOY SAYS

"WHY DON'T THEY BUILD MORE WISHING WELLS?"

LITTLE ARTIST BOY SAYS

"'Please Follow the Highlighted Route', I will, but, I have to say, it DOES NOT look like a GOOD route"

LITTLE ARTIST BOY SAYS

"Work helps me forget"

LITTLE ARTIST BOY
SAYS

"You say 'unexpected item in bagging area', sorry, but that's my other shopping from a cheaper shop (WHICH WOULDN'T BE DIFFICULT... THESE PRICES ARE WAY OUTTA LINE!)"

LITTLE ARTIST BOY SAYS

"CONTRACTS MAKE MOST PEOPLE ANXIOUS"

LITTLE ARTIST BOY SAYS

"Keep all your bank statements (some day you're gonna thank me for this advice)"

"Normal service will be resumed... at some point... in the future... someone, I forget who, told me"

LITTLE ARTIST BOY SAYS

"A SMOCK & A BERET ALWAYS LOOK PRETTY FRESH 'N' FLY"

LITTLE ARTIST BOY
SAYS

"SOME DAYS
it helps to shout
'I don't know
why I bother'
& break into
an elaborate
tap dance"

erm...

DIFFICULT CONVERSATIONS

LITTLE ARTIST BOY
SAYS

"CALL IT OUT FOR WHAT IT IS!!!!....... O.K. THEN... IT'S A SUPER-LAZY-SLUG-FEST!!!"

LITTLE ARTIST BOY SAYS

"There goes that unnecessarily aggressive individual... Oh hey! Hi there!"

"They say 'GOD HATES A COWARD' but I think most people probably hate a coward"

LITTLE ARTIST BOY SAYS

"If the subject turns to politics, say 'you have to remember that, in **politics**, if you haven't got the numbers, you have to decide what you're prepared to compromise on'"

LITTLE ARTIST BOY SAYS

"You know that person who would start a fight with a paper bag in an empty room? That person is most probably related to me... in fact, they ARE definitely related to me, want to make something of it? WELL DO YA?"

HEALTHY BODY, HEALTHY MIND

LITTLE ARTIST BOY
SAYS

"GIMME CARBS"

LITTLE ARTIST BOY SAYS

"THERE'S A LOT TO BE SAID FOR WANDERING"

LITTLE ARTIST BOY SAYS

"ARGHHHHHHHHH!"

LITTLE ARTIST BOY SAYS

"Don't give up, never give up"

"I cannot help you today as I am experiencing COMLETE & UTTER BRAIN FOG"

LITTLE ARTIST BOY SAYS

"Bring out the Bromley in me!"

"STOP ME
& ASK ABOUT
MY TIDYING!.........

NO, THEY WON'T,
COS IT'S BORING"

LITTLE ARTIST BOY SAYS

"I WILL DO IT, IF I CAN BE BOTHERED"

LITTLE ARTIST BOY SAYS

"If you FEEL sick ... BE sick"

LITTLE ARTIST BOY SAYS

"Dance that mood off"

"Some days I'm in CONSUMER HEAVEN, other days I cannot tolerate a single shop without feeling sick & ill"

LOVE
& RELATIONSHIPS

"'Your money is OUR MONEY but MY money is MY money' this is worth remembering if you ever get married"

LITTLE ARTIST BOY SAYS

"CELEBRATE RESTLESS SOULS & THEN ... HAVE A REST"

LITTLE ARTIST BOY
SAYS

"Imperfect is my perfect"

"Not everything is about YOU, most things are, I'll grant you that"

LITTLE ARTIST BOY SAYS

"Just remember if you answer THAT person's text the noise will start right back up"

LITTLE ARTIST BOY SAYS

"I Love Warhol Forever"

LITTLE ARTIST BOY SAYS

"They say it all started with Les Demoiselles d'Avignon"

LITTLE ARTIST BOY
SAYS

"There is not one thing I do not like about you"

MAKING CONNECTIONS & SOCIAL EXCELLENCE

LITTLE ARTIST BOY SAYS

"DON'T TELL TALES OUT OF SCHOOL"

LITTLE ARTIST BOY

"Swerve from macho"

LITTLE ARTIST BOY
SAYS

"My mum is good at testing wether a pot of cream is 'on the turn' but you must allow her to repeat the phrase 'just a minute! just a minute!' About 100 times then, it's all systems GO"

LITTLE ARTIST BOY SAYS

"Good manners never went out of fashion, thank you & Good Evening"

LITTLE ARTIST BOY SAYS

"If there's a bandwagon... jump on it!"

LITTLE ARTIST BOY
SAYS

"If someone you loathe walks past, say in a loud voice 'I heard their fiscal policy framework was under review'"

(I don't know either but I CAN guarantee they will be impressed)

LITTLE ARTIST BOY
SAYS

"STAND AT
THE BACK...
AND HOPE...
NO ONE WILL NOTICE"
(P.S. YOU CAN SLIP AWAY INTO
THE NIGHT MORE EASILY TOO)

LITTLE ARTIST BOY SAYS

"Laterzzzzz"